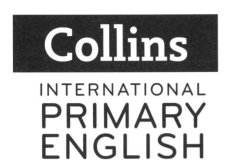

Collins

INTERNATIONAL
PRIMARY
ENGLISH

Workbook 1

William Collins' dream of knowledge for all began with the publication of his firstbookin1819. A self-educated mill worker, he not only enriched millions of lives, but also founded a flourishing publishing house. Today, staying true to this spirit, Collins books are packed with inspiration, innovation and practical expertise. They place you at the centre of a world of possibility and give you exactly what you need to explore it.

Collins. Freedom to teach.

Published by Collins
An imprint of HarperCollins*Publishers*
The News Building
1 London Bridge Street
London SE1 9GF

Macken House, 39/40 Mayor Street Upper, Dublin 1, DO1 C9W8, Ireland

Browse the complete Collins catalogue at
www.collins.co.uk

© HarperCollins*Publishers* Limited 2021

10 9 8 7 6

ISBN 978-0-00-836769-5

British Library Cataloguing-in-Publication Data
A catalogue record for this publication is available from the British Library.

Author: Joyce Vallar
Series editor: Daphne Paizee
Publisher: Elaine Higgleton
Product developer: Natasha Paul
Project manager: Karen Williams
Development editor: Sonya Newland
Copyeditor: Karen Williams
Proofreader: Catherine Dakin
Cover designer: Gordon MacGilp

Cover illustrator: Petr Horácek
Internal designer and typesetter: Ken Vail Graphic Design Ltd.
Text permissions researcher: Rachel Thorne
Image permissions researcher: Alison Prior
Illustrators: Ken Vail Graphic Design Ltd., Advocate Art, Beehive Illustration and QBS Learning
Production controller: Lyndsey Rogers
Printed in Great Britain by Martins the Printers

Third-party websites, publications and resources referred to in this publication have not been endorsed by Cambridge Assessment International Education.

With thanks to the following teachers and schools for reviewing materials in development: Amanda DuPratt, Shreyaa Dutta Gupta, Sharmila Majumdar, Sushmita Ray and Sukanya Singhal, Calcutta International School; Akash Raut, DSB International School, Mumbai; Melissa Brobst, International School of Budapest; Shalini Reddy, Manthan International School; Taman Rama Intercultural School.

Acknowledgements
The publishers gratefully acknowledge the permissions granted to reproduce copyright material in the book. Every effort has been made to contact the holders of copyright material, but if any have been inadvertently overlooked, the Publisher will be pleased to make the necessary arrangements at the first opportunity.

Cover illustration: *The Lonely Penguin* Reprinted by permission of HarperCollins Publishers Ltd © 2011 Petr Horácek. *The Big Red Bus* Reprinted by permission of HarperCollins*Publishers* Ltd © 2006 Alison Hawes, illustrated by Woody Fox; *Bot on the Moon* Reprinted by permission of HarperCollins*Publishers* Ltd © 2006 Shoo Rayner; *Funny Fish* Reprinted by permission of HarperCollins*Publishers* Ltd © 2005 Michaela Morgan, illustrated by Jon Stuart; *The Small Bun* Reprinted by permission of HarperCollins*Publishers* Ltd © 2006 Martin Waddell, illustrated by T. S. Spookytooth; *The Lonely Penguin* Reprinted by permission of HarperCollins*Publishers* Ltd © 2011 Petr Horácek.

We are grateful to the following for permission to reproduce copyright material:
Grace Andreacchi for the poem on p.29 'Mister Moon' from *Little poems for children* copyright © Grace Andreacchi; Joyce Vallor for the poem on p.34 'A Fine Feathered Fish' by Joyce Vallar from *Hector Hedgehog's Big Book of Rhymes*, Collins Fun Phonics, copyright © Joyce Vallar.

The publishers wish to thank the following for permission to reproduce photographs. Every effort has been made to trace copyright holders and to obtain their permission for the use of copyright materials. The publishers will gladly receive any information enabling them to rectify any error or omission at the first opportunity.
(t = top, c = centre, b = bottom, r = right, l = left)
p1c ghrzuzudu/Shutterstock, p18tl karnoff/Shutterstock, p18tr Memo Angeles/Shutterstock, p18bl ghrzuzudu/Shutterstock, p18br Volha Shaukavets/Shutterstock, p20 Eric Isselee/ Shutterstock, p21l, cl, Eric Isselee/Shutterstock, p21cr Alex Stemmer/Shutterstock, Ray Kemensky/Shutterstock, p22bl Vladimir Chernyanskiy/Shutterstock, p23t Piotr Wawrzyniuk/ Shutterstock, p23b Aleksei Verhovski/Shutterstock, p37tl Ozgur Coskun/Shutterstock, p37tcl JIANG HONGYAN/Shutterstock, p37bcl Jiang Zhongyan/Shutterstock, p37bl Edward Westmacott/Shutterstock, p37tr Azdora/Shutterstock, p37tcr rangizzz/Shutterstock, p37bcr holbox/Shutterstock, p37br Angorius/Shutterstock.

MIX
Paper | Supporting
responsible forestry
FSC™ C007454

This book is produced from independently certified FSC™ paper to ensure responsible forest management.

For more information visit: www.harpercollins.co.uk/green

Contents

1 Going places

Vocabulary: transport words Student's Book page 1

Match the words to the pictures.

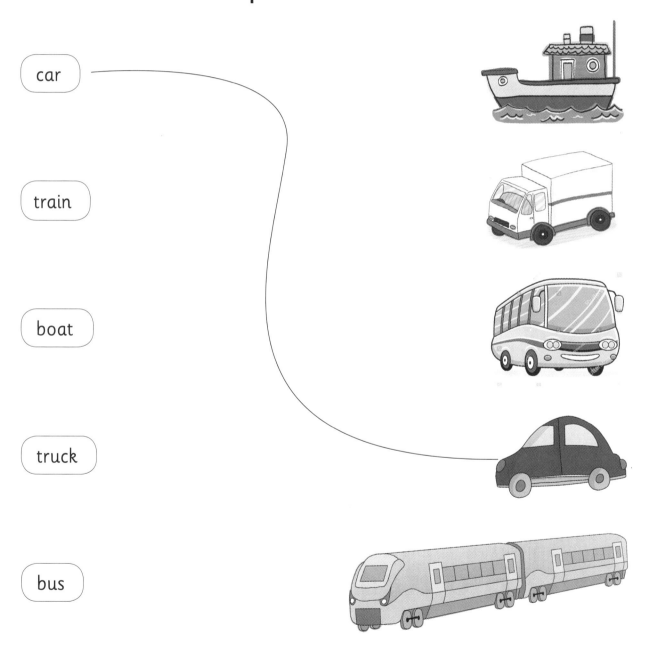

car

train

boat

truck

bus

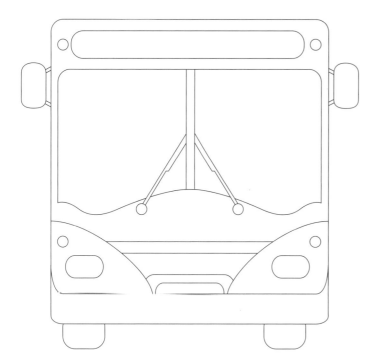

1 Draw a bus stop.

2 Draw three people waiting for the bus.

3 On the front of the bus, write where it is going.

4 Colour the bus.

5 Copy the book title.

The Big Red Bus

_____

1 Match the beginning of each sentence with its ending.

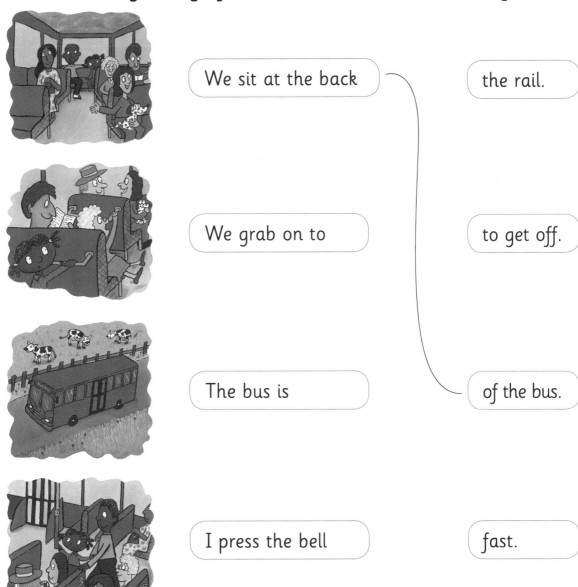

We sit at the back   the rail.

We grab on to   to get off.

The bus is   of the bus.

I press the bell   fast.

2 Write the whole sentence that starts with the word 'I'.

_____

1 **Read the words in the box.**

| did | red | big | bed |

● Write the two words that describe the
  bus in the story.

_____   _____

2 **Read the words in the box.**

| bus stop | clock | bell | duck pond |

● Use the words in the box to label each picture.

   _____clock_____

   _____

   _____

   _____

3 **Complete the sentences. Choose the right word.**

● The bus is _____.

| red | yellow |

● The bus is at the bus _____.

| stop | shop |

Student's Book page 9

Choose the word to match the picture. Write the word.

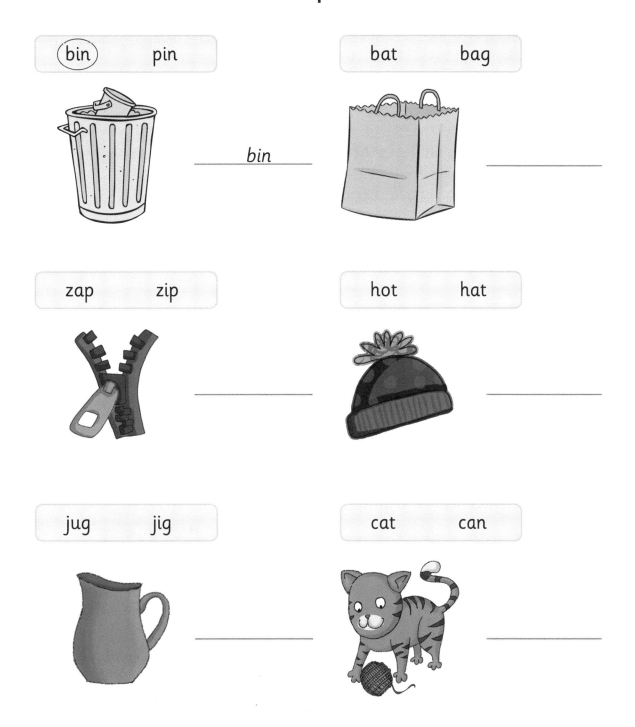

bin   pin

____bin____

bat   bag

_____

zap   zip

_____

hot   hat

_____

jug   jig

_____

cat   can

_____

5

1 **Read the words in the box.**

tug	fan	get	hug
pet	man	bug	tan
rug	set	can	met

2 **Write the words in lists of rhyming words.**

jug   pan   net

tug _____   _____   _____

_____   _____   _____

_____   _____   _____

_____   _____   _____

3 **Read and complete the funny poem.**

Dan, Dan, the funny old man

Washed his face in the frying _____

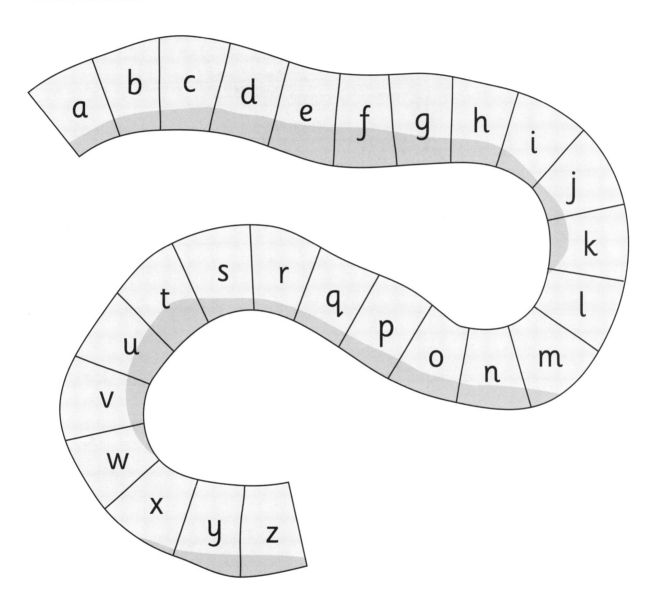

1 **Answer the questions about the alphabet.**

● How many letters are in the alphabet? _____

● Circle the vowels in the alphabet above.

● How many vowels are in the alphabet? _____

Write the vowels. _____ _____ _____ _____ _____

2 Fill in the letters of the alphabet to join the bus stops.
Colour all the vowels red.

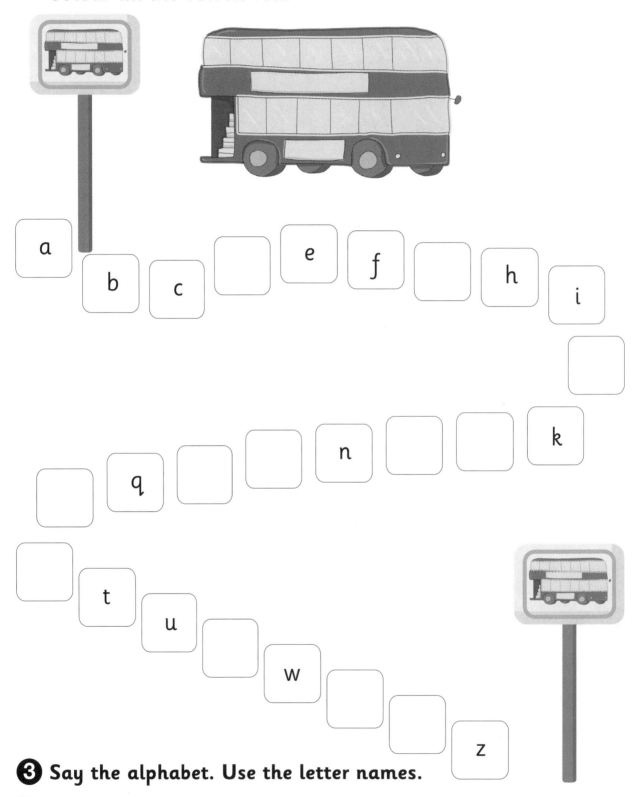

a

b

c

e

f

h

i

k

n

q

t

u

w

z

3 Say the alphabet. Use the letter names.

Put a vowel in the box. Write the word under the box like this.

a e i o u

b a g
___bag___

p ⬜ t
_____

l ⬜ d
_____

j ⬜ g
_____

n ⬜ t
_____

h ⬜ t
_____

l ⬜ g
_____

z ⬜ p
_____

s ⬜ n
_____

10

t ⬜ n
_____

2 Having fun

Reading and writing Student's Book page 11

1 PAIR WORK. Write your name and your partner's name in the chart.

2 Draw pictures.

	Me _____	My partner _____
My favourite thing to do at school to keep fit.		
My favourite thing to do at home to keep fit.		

1 Tick (✓) the things that Dev likes to do.

Dev likes running to get fit.

Dev likes running with a cap and a map.

Dev likes hopping to get fit.

Dev likes hopping on top of a box.

Dev likes hopping on a rug.

Dev likes jogging with a fish on a dish.

2 Circle the words in question 1 that end with –*ing*.

3 Write one thing that Rev likes to do.

Student's Book pages 12–14

1 **Make sentences about Rev and Dev.**

Rev and Dev
Dev can run
Rev can hop
Dev can jog

for fun to get fit.
with a fish on a dish.
like to play in the sun.
on a rug.

2 **Make more sentences about Rev and Dev.**

Rev can run
Dev can hop
Rev can hop
Rev and Dev have fun

in the mud in the sun.
with a cap and a map.
with a jug and a mug.
on the top of a box.

1 Can you do these things? Write 'can' or 'cannot'.

I _____ swim well.

I _____ climb a tree.

I _____ ride a bike.

I _____ run fast.

2 Write about what you can do.

_____

_____

_____

_____

Student's Book page 18

1 Write the word for each picture.

 _____

 _____

10 _____

 _____

 _____

 _____

 _____

 _____

2 Read the words in question 1.

Write the words in rhyming pairs.

_____ and _____   _____ and _____

_____ and _____   _____ and _____

The alphabet | Alphabet

1 Circle the capital letters.

T   a   D   y   c   F   G   m

P   r   B   N   H   h   n   M

B   R   S   b   W   f   Z   u

2 Match the lower case letters to their capitals.

a	D	n	P
b	E	o	Q
c	A	p	N
d	B	q	O
e	C	r	T
f	G	s	R
g	H	t	U
h	F	u	S
i	J	v	Z
j	K	w	X
k	M	x	V
l	L	y	W
m	I	z	Y

Rev liked carrying two things at the same time.

1 Write the word 'and' three times.

_____   _____   _____

2 Add –*and* to each letter. Say the new word out loud.

b _____band_____   l _____

h _____   s _____

3 Add –*end* to each letter. Say the new word out loud.

s _____send_____   l _____

b _____   m _____

fish

dish

1 **What sound do you hear at the end of the two words above?**

● Write the two letters that make the sound. _____

2 **Read the words in the box. Find the *sh* sounds.**

shop	dish	shed	shut
wish	rush	ship	mash
fish	shell	rash	hush

● Circle in **red** the words beginning with the *sh* sound.

● Circle in **blue** the words ending with the *sh* sound.

3 **Write the word for each picture. Choose the word from the box in question 2.**

_____ _____ _____

3 Let's find out

1 Make up a title for each of the books.

2 Write your title on the cover.

Sounds and spelling
Student's Book page 23

Add –ng or –ck to match the word to the picture.

ng or **ck**

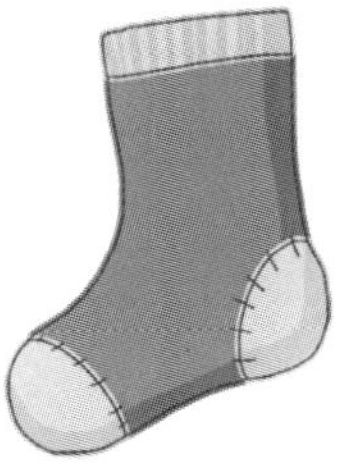

so __ck__

si _____

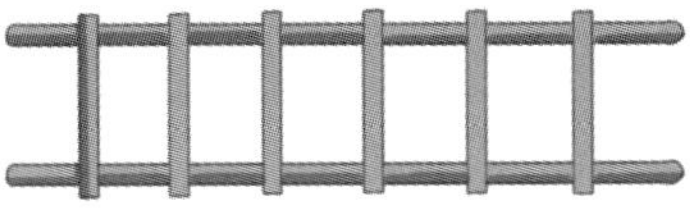

tra _____

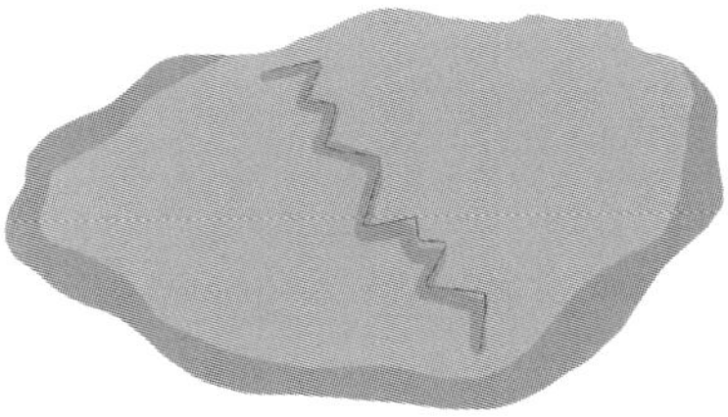

cra _____

tru _____

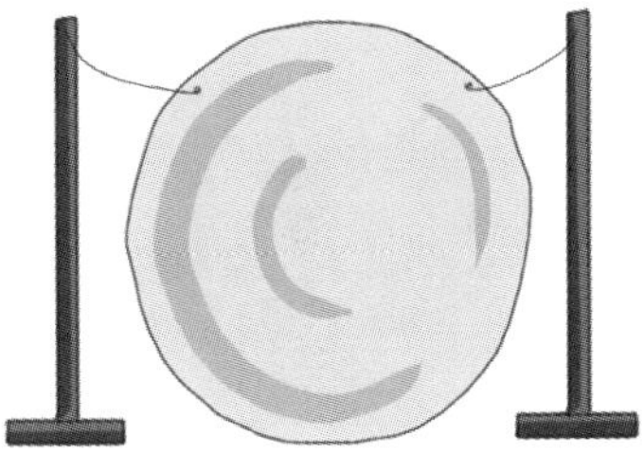

go _____

swi _____

lo _____

ri _____

Read the words in the box. Use the words to label the parts of the fox.

long bushy tail   large ears   black eyes

sharp claws   fur   pointed snout

Look at the chart.

Name the animals that have legs. _____

_____

Name the animal that has feathers. _____

Name the animal that has antlers. _____

Name the animals that have a tail. _____

_____

	fox	owl	snake	deer
legs	✓	✓		✓
feathers		✓		
antlers				✓
tail	✓	✓	✓	✓

1 **Read the names of the animals in the box.**
Find the words in the word search.

~~lion~~ duck cat fox camel deer owl tiger

c	z	m	d	u	c	k
a	l	y	e	j	a	t
t	i	g	e	r	m	h
f	o	x	r	w	e	s
b	n	k	o	w	l	n

2 **Tick (✓) the sentence that describes the picture.**

There are two foxes. ☐   The cat is playing. ☐
There is one fox. ☐   The cats are playing. ☐

Make sentences about the ducks and lions.

Ducks

Lions

have feathers.

live in the jungle.

have beaks.

are birds.

roar.

have webbed feet.

belong to the cat family.

can run fast.

4 The moon

Join the alphabet letters to make the picture.
Start at 'a' and go to 'z'.

1 Read the labels on the items in the shop window.

2 Write a shopping list for Bot.

Shopping list

Student's Book pages 32–34

Match the beginning of each sentence with its ending.

Bot zoomed past	with Mum.
He sent	Bot on his hat.
Bot was back	on the moon.
Bot was on	all the twinkling stars.
The club hit	the card to his mum.
Bot landed	a trip to the moon.

Circle the correct ending. Write the word.

lk   sk

_____

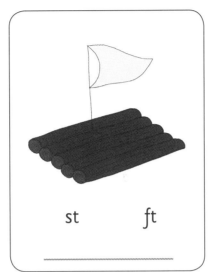

st   ft

_____

ft   st

_____

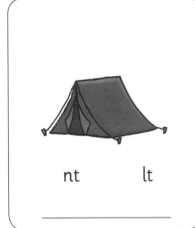

nt   lt

_____

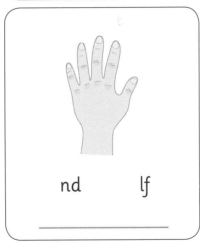

nd   lf

_____

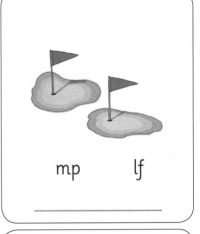

mp   lf

_____

lt   nt

_____

nd   lf

_____

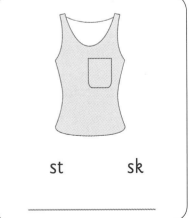

st   sk

_____

Complete the sentences.

1 Bot was on a _____ to the moon.

2 _____ off! Woosh!

3 His rocket was _____.

4 Bot zoomed _____ all the twinkling stars.

5 He _____ the card to his mum.

6 It said, "Having a good _____."

Student's Book page 40

| Mister Moon! Good night! | to follow me? |
| Mister Moon! Hello! | with his big bright eye. |

Use the words in each box once to make the poem rhyme.

Mister Moon

Mister Moon looks out of the sky

And watches me _____

And follows me wherever I go

Hello, _____

Of all the children that he can see

Why does he choose _____

And watch me with his eye so bright

Good night, _____

5 Funny Fish

Match the beginning of each sentence with its ending.

Three funny fish were	as bright as the sun!"
"I am bright	and funny and red."
That was the end	swimming in the sea.
"I am yellow –	like a stone."
"I can look	of the funny red fish.
"The big bad fish	leaves me alone!"

30

1 Write what is happening in each picture.

2 Check that your sentences have a capital letter and a full stop.

1 **Read each word aloud.**

said   came   were   Then   was

● Find the words above in the story.

● Write the page(s) each word is on in the book.

said   page(s) _____

came   page(s) _____

were   page(s) _____

then   page(s) _____

was   page(s) _____

2 **Use the words above to complete the sentences.**

● Then along _____ the big fish.

● It _____ , "No one ever looks at me."

● Three funny fish _____ swimming in the sea.

● That _____ the end of the funny red fish.

● _____ the big fish came and… Yum, yum, yum!

Student's Book page 48

Change the vowel sounds to make new words.

a   e   i   o   u

Like this:

e	➡	u	o	➡	a
rest	➡	*rust*	lost	➡	_____
a	➡	u	u	➡	a
lamp	➡	_____	dump	➡	_____
a	➡	e	e	➡	a
sand	➡	_____	bend	➡	_____
a	➡	e	e	➡	o
past	➡	_____	left	➡	_____

Use the line endings to complete the poem.

| five furry fins | four fishy tins. | out of those tins! |

A Fine Feathered Fish

A fine feathered fish

With _____

Falls onto a dish

Next to _____

This fine feathered fish

With _____

Yells "Quick!" to those fish

"Come _____ "

The alphabet | Alphabet

Join the alphabet letters to make the picture.

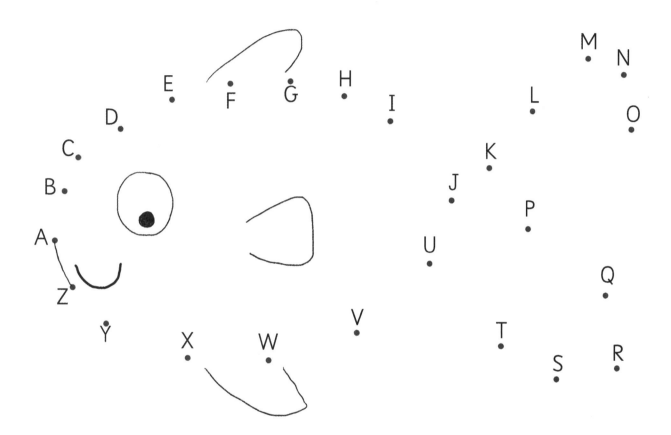

6 Food

Read the headings. List four foods that belong to each food group.

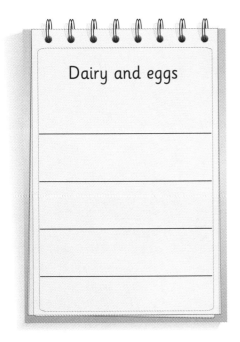

Dairy and eggs

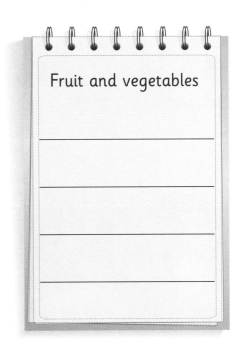

Fruit and vegetables

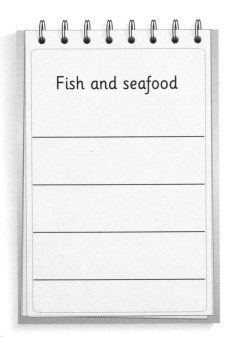

Fish and seafood

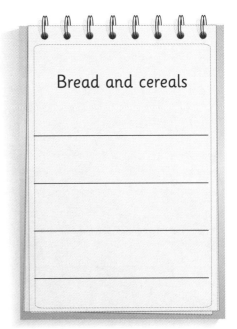

Bread and cereals

Tick (✓) the correct word to label each picture. Then write the word.

crab

octopus

_____

lobster

eel

_____

prawn

octopus

_____

shrimp

tuna

_____

squid

crab

_____

tuna

lobster

_____

crab

lobster

_____

eel

mussels

_____

chop

eat

mix

peel

Use the sentence starters to write instructions for making a fruit salad.

First _____

Next _____

Then _____

Last of all _____

Sounds and spelling | Phonics

Use the letters in the boxes to make rhyming words.

| h | p | st |

cuff

huff

puff

stuff

| m | dr | pr |

less

| gl | br | cl |

pass

| b | w | s | sm |

tell

| p | sp | fr | st |

hill

| t | m | b | l |

cross

1 Draw the food.

2 Write signs to show what people can buy.

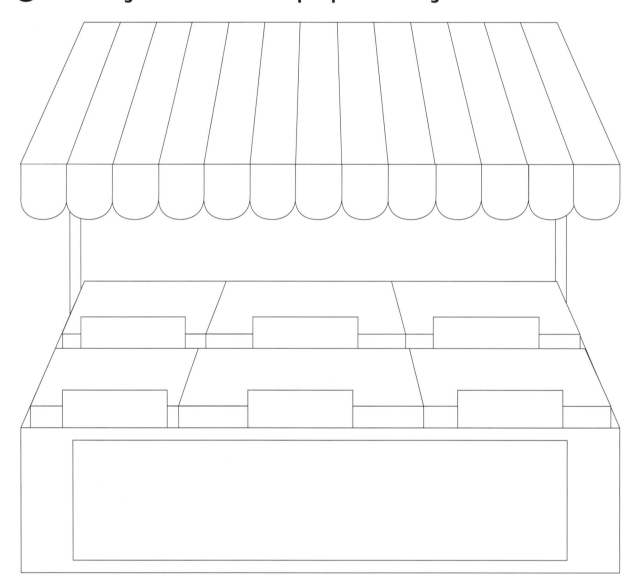

3 Write a name on the stall. Colour in your picture.

❶ **On the plate, draw a healthy meal that you would like to eat. Label your drawing.**

❷ **Decorate the plate with a pattern.**

7 Traditional stories

Reading and writing Student's Book pages 62–64

Who said this?

Draw a line to match each sentence to the correct picture.

"I am too fast for the man and his wife."

"You have beaten me."

"Trust me."

"If I get on your back, you will eat me!"

"To eat you!"

"Why have you stopped?"

"Get on my back and I will carry you across the river."

1 Read the words in the box. Make sentences with the words in the box.

A   a   The   the

- _____ small bun sat at _____ table.
- _____ peach was on _____ table.
- _____ small bun ate _____ peach.
- _____ peach had _____ big stone.

2 Read the words in the box. Make sentences with the words in the box.

his   the   said   for   you

"I am too fast _____ the man and _____ wife, and the sheep and _____ goat, and I am too fast for _____!"

_____ the bun.

Look at the pictures. Fill in the missing letters. Choose from

ee   or   **oa**

Then write the words for the pictures.

g_____ o a _____ l

f_____t

_____

r_____d

p_____l

_____

h_____l

t_____d

_____

tr_____

g_____t

_____

1 **Imagine you are the small bun. Write your story.**

A hungry _____

baked me.

I hopped off the

_____ and ran.

First I met a hungry

_____.

Next I met a hungry

_____.

Then I met a cunning

_____.

The fox said, "Get on my

_____."

I got on the back of the

_____.

The fox ate _____.

2 **Read your story aloud. Check. Does it make sense?**

1 How did the man and his wife feel when the small bun ran away? Tick (✓) the words.

happy	☐	worried	☐	hungry	☐
sad	☐	excited	☐	cross	☐
surprised	☐	angry	☐	pleased	☐

2 Draw a picture of the man and his wife when the small bun hopped off the dish.

1 Think of a different ending for the story. Draw a picture to show your new ending.

2 Write your new ending for the story

8 Feelings

Circle the words that end with –ed.

Match the beginning of each sentence with its ending.

Penguin (climbed)   with his friends.

Penguin looked   up the hill.

Penguin laughed   for his friends.

Penguin splashed   into the air.

Penguin jumped   in the cold water.

48

Student's Book page 77

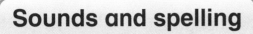

oo   or   ee

Look at the pictures. Write the words.

_____

_____

7 days in a
_____

_____

_____

_____

_____

_____

_____

Sounds and spelling   Student's Book page 77

Crunch, crunch! Penguin's running through the snow.

1 Say the word 'snow'.

- What sound do you hear at the end of the word 'snow'?
- What letters make the sound?
- Write the letters. _____

2 Add –ow to make new words. Write the words.

gr _____	sl _____
bl _____	gl _____
fl _____	thr _____

3 Write the words under the correct picture.

pillow	window	rainbow

_____   _____   _____

1 Imagine that you are the penguin. Complete your story.

I was looking for _____.

I ran through the _____.

I slid on the _____.

I looked _____.

I climbed up the _____.

I jumped into _____.

SPLASH!

I found _____.

2 Read your story aloud. Check. Does it make sense?

Listening and speaking Student's Book page 78

Penguin felt lonely when he was looking for his friends.

PAIR WORK.

❶ Talk about how Penguin felt when he found his friends.

❷ What makes you happy?

Writing Student's Book page 78

Write six things round the happy face that make you happy.

Draw a poster to help anyone who is lonely know that they have a friend.

9 Life lessons

Reading and writing   Student's Book pages 81–83

1 Look at the cover. What do you think you will read about
in the book? Circle your answers.

spiders	a turtle
food	a party
friends	turtles
	a spider

2 Write the plural of these words from the story.
Then read the words out loud.

spider _____

turtle _____

hand _____

coat _____

hat _____

visitor _____

3 Find words ending in –s and –ed in *Anansi and Turtle*.
Write the picture number and the word like this:

● Picture 1 visitors
● Picture 2 opened

Student's Book page 88

1 Read these words from the poem about the mice on page 88 of the Student's Book.

> nice   mouse   too   house   stew   mice

2 Which words rhyme? List them below.

- _____*mouse*_____ rhymes with _____*house*_____
- _____ rhymes with _____
- _____ rhymes with _____

3 PAIR WORK. Make your own lists of words that rhyme.

meal	make	light

4 PAIR WORK. Read your lists out loud to your partner.

Match the beginning of each sentence with its ending.

"You were too slow	visitors at dinner time.
Anansi did not like	the door.
Anansi opened	to eat the food.
Turtle went	sat down to dinner.
Anansi began	to wash his hands.
"Why did you	and I was hungry."
Anansi the spider	not wait for me?"

Student's Book page 82

Read the invitation. Write the answers to the questions.

Invitation
To: Anansi
Please come
to dinner.
Place: At the pond
Time: 5 o'clock
From: Turtle

● Who got the invitation?

_____

● Who sent the invitation?

_____

● Where should Anansi go for dinner?

_____

● What time is the dinner?

_____

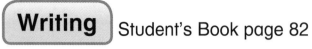

Make an invitation.

Invitation

Please come to _____

To _____

Place _____

Date _____

Time _____

From _____

1 Write the capital letter for each letter. Say the name as you write each letter.

A a	B b	___ c	___ d	___ e	
___ f	___ g	___ h	___ i	___ j	
___ k	___ l	___ m	___ n	___ o	
___ p	___ q	___ r	___ s	___ t	
___ u	___ v	___ w	___ x	___ y	___ z

2 These names should have capital letters at the beginning. Write the names correctly.

   rev

_____

   shoo rayner

_____

   nut hill

_____

   dev

_____

   joe's bakery

_____

   bot

_____

How well did I do?

■ I did OK   ● I did well   ▲ I did really well

Unit	■	●	▲
1 Going places			
2 Having fun			
3 Let's find out			
4 The moon			
5 *Funny Fish*			
6 Food			
7 Traditional stories			
8 Feelings			
9 Life lessons			